SHUT UP DEVIL, IT IS WRITTEN

SHUT UP DEVIL, IT IS WRITTEN

Spiritual Warfare

Combatting Real Life Thoughts, with Real Truth

BY KARIM Z. HENRY

SHUT UP DEVIL, IT IS WRITTEN

November Media Publishing
Copyright © 2021 Karim Z. Henry

For permission requests, write to the author, addressed "attention: KARIM Z. HENRY" at the email address below.

Karimzahir@yahoo.com

Ordering information: special discounts are available on quantity purchases by corporations, associations, and others. For details, contact the author at the email address above.

Printed in the United States of America
Published & Produced by November Media Publishing

All Scriptures quotations, unless otherwise indicated, are taken from the New American Standard Bible (NASB), King James Version, CJB, Voice, RSV, EXB.

ISBN-13: 979-8-9852149-3-2

"**Find HIS Truth in your season.**"

~Karim Z. Henry

CONTENTS

FROM THE AUTHOR

This book is dedicated to my siblings in the faith who undergo the same persecution, sufferings, and afflictions throughout the world. Remember to be of good cheer and count it all joy. Add this book to your weaponry. God sees you, and HE will avenge you speedily.

As it is written, so resist him, firm in your faith, knowing that the same experiences of suffering are being accomplished by your brothers and sisters who are in the world.

1 Peter 5:9

FOREWORD

We're in a war! But the good news is we have already won. One may ask, if we already won the war, then what are we fighting? We're fighting the good fight of faith, according to Apostle Paul in 1st Timothy. Faith in what? Faith that we already won the war. This may be mind-boggling or even a tongue twister for some, but it's true. We're contending for the faith that we're already victorious in every area of our lives. Brothers and sisters, our adversary is heating the furnace seven times hotter. The issue is that our enemy is not as conspicuous as a boxer in a boxing ring, yet the fight is just as real and fierce. Breaking News! The battlefield is not in a boxing ring but in your mind. Since the battle is in your mind, then we must equip ourselves with spiritual armor. We may be fighting a good fight, but it's a fight, nonetheless. Therefore, take a journey with me to study our opponent and detect his schemes, wiles, and tactics. We'll strengthen our spiritual shoulders to raise the shield of faith against the fiery darts of the enemy. And we'll learn how to wield the sword of the spirit, which is the word of God, in order to keep our adversary on the run.

"Protect yourself against our enemy's fiery darts (thoughts). Be sure to put on your helmet (salvation), raise your shield (faith), and wield your sword (The Word of God)".

~Karim Z. Henry

Thought: This is as far as you'll go. Answer: Shut Up Devil, it is written...

That the Lord shall increase me more and more, my children and me, it is written that His righteousness is revealed from faith to faith and that He is the author and finisher (developer) of my faith. It is written that He knows the thoughts that He thinks towards me, thoughts of peace and not evil, to give me hope in my outcome and bring me to an expected end. My future is so bright, so much so that it is written that my eyes have not seen, nor have my ears heard, nor has it entered my heart the things HE has prepared for me. In Jesus' Name. Amen!

SCRIPTURE REFERENCES

Romans 1:17, 1 Corinthians 2:9 Hebrews 12:2, Jeremiah 29:11

Thought: You are broke now, and you'll always be broke.
Answer: Shut Up Devil, it is written...

That wealth and riches shall fill my house and that my God shall supply all my needs according to His riches in Glory in Christ Jesus. It is written that whatsoever things that I desire, when I pray and when I believe that I receive them, that He will give them. He will give me Grace and Glory, and no good thing will He withhold from me or anyone who walks uprightly. It is written that I will eat the fruit of the labor of my hands and that I'll be blessed. All will be well with me because My God is able to make all grace (every favor and earthly blessing) come to me in abundance so that I will always and under all circumstances be self-sufficient. I will possess enough to require no aid or support and be furnished in abundance for every good work and charitable donation. He will do it. My God will give me seeds for my sowing and bread for my eating and will also provide and multiply my [resources for] sowing and increase the fruits of my righteousness, which manifests itself in active goodness, kindness, and charity. Since I am willing and obedient, I shall eat the good of the land. In Jesus' Name. Amen!

SCRIPTURE REFERENCES

Psalms 112:3, Mark 11:24, Psalms 84:11, Psalms 128:2, 2 Corinthians 9:8;10, Philippians 4:19, Isaiah 1:19

Thought: God is Angry with you for all you've done.
Answer: Shut Up Devil, it is written...

That there is no condemnation to them which are in Christ Jesus. I AM in Christ, and I have a covenant with God who swore to me that He would never be angry with me nor rebuke me. It is written that He will be merciful to my unrighteousness and that my sins and iniquity He will remember no more. He has compassion on me and will trample all my sins under His feet and toss them into the depths of the sea. Jesus, who knew no sin, was made my sin offering once and for all. Because of this, I was made the righteousness of God in him. Because of Christ Jesus, God has made unto me wisdom, righteousness, sanctification, and redemption. It is written that righteousness was imputed unto me because I believe in Him who raised Jesus, my Lord, from the dead. In Jesus' Name. Amen!

SCRIPTURE REFERENCES

Romans 8:1, Isaiah 54:9, Hebrews 8:12, Micah 7:19, 2 Corinthians 5:21 1 Corinthian 1:30 Romans 4:24.

Thought: God doesn't really love you. Answer: Shut Up Devil, it is written...

That God shows his love for me that while I was still sinning, Christ died for us. God will rejoice over me with joy. He will rest in His love towards me and make no mention [of past sins, or even recall them]; He will exult over me with singing. It is written that God so loved the world, that he gave his only Son, that whoever believes in him should not perish but have eternal life. God is love, and whoever abides in love abides in God, and God abides in him. It is written that God is merciful and gracious, slow to anger and abounding in steadfast love and faithfulness. I'm confident that neither death nor life, nor angels nor rulers, nor things present nor things to come, nor powers, nor height nor depth, nor anything else in all creation, will be able to separate me from the love of God in Christ Jesus our Lord. God loves me with an everlasting love. In Jesus' Name. Amen!

SCRIPTURE REFERENCES

John 3:16, Romans 5:8, Zephaniah 3:17, 1 John 4:16
Romans 8:38-39 Psalms 86:15 Jeremiah 31:3

Thought: Death is near you.
Answer: Shut Up Devil, it is written...

That He will satisfy me with long life and show me His salvation, God is patient toward me, not wishing that I should perish but that I should reach repentance. And If I confess my sins, he is faithful and just to forgive me of my sins, and cleanse me from all unrighteousness. Therefore, I will not fear those who kill the body but cannot kill the soul. But I will fear him who can destroy both soul and body in hell. It is written that everyone who lives and believes in Him shall never die. The dust will return to the earth as it was, and the spirit returns to God who gave it. Therefore, for me, to live is Christ, and to die is gain. In Jesus' Name. Amen!

SCRIPTURE REFERENCES

Psalms 91:16, 2 Peter 3:9, Matthew 10:28, John 11:26
Ecclesiastes 12:7 1 John 1:9 Philippians 1:21

Thought: You're the same old person. Answer: Shut Up Devil, it is written...

That if any man is in Christ, he is a new creature. I am in Christ, and old things are passed away, and all things become new. My old man was crucified with Christ. And it is written that if I am dead with Christ, I believe that I shall also live with him. He delivered me from the power of darkness and has translated me into the kingdom of his dear Son. In whom I have redemption through his blood, even the forgiveness of sins. It is written I am of a chosen generation, a royal priest-hood, a holy nation, a peculiar child handpicked by God as his very own elect. Get thee behind me, Satan. How dare you accuse me whom God has chosen for his own? God him-self has given me right standing with Him. I have been born again. Born of God and grafted into the family of God as a seed of Abraham and heir according to the promise. In Jesus' Name. Amen!

SCRIPTURE REFERENCES

2 Corinthians 5:17, Romans 6:6 Colossians 1:13-14,
1 Peter 2:9, Isaiah 42:1, Romans 8:33, Matthew 16:23,
1 John 5:1. Romans 11:17, Galatians 3:29.

Thought: You're not really healed. Do you feel healed?
Answer: Shut Up Devil, it is written...

That the just shall live by faith and not by sight or appearance. My feelings have nothing to do with it. Only what God said, get thee behind me, Satan. God is not a man, so he does not lie. He is not human, so he does not change his mind. Has he ever spoken and failed to act? Has he ever promised and not carried it through? God forbids! He bore my sins in His own body on the tree, that I, being dead to sins, should live unto righteousness: by whose stripes I was healed. He bore it all! It is written that He has borne my griefs (sicknesses, weaknesses, and distresses) and carried my sorrows and pains [of punishment]. For this He was wounded for my transgressions, He was bruised for my guilt and iniquities; the chastisement of my peace and well-being was upon Him, and with the stripes that wounded Him, I was healed and made whole. In Jesus' Name. Amen!

SCRIPTURE REFERENCES

2 Corinthians 5:7, Numbers 23:19, Matthew 16:23,
1 Peter 2:24, Isaiah 53:4-5,

Thought: You're not strong enough. Answer: Shut Up Devil, it is written...

That I have strength for all things in Christ, who empowers me. I am self-sufficient in Christ's sufficiency. It is written that His Grace is sufficient for me. His strength is made perfect in my weakness. Therefore, I will boast more gladly about my weaknesses so that Christ's power may rest on me. For when I am weak, then I am strong. It is not written for me to be strong of myself. But it is written for me to be strong in the Lord and the power of his might. He will strengthen me; He will help me, and He will uphold me with His righteous right hand. In Jesus' Name. Amen!

SCRIPTURE REFERENCES

2 Corinthians 12:9-10, Philippians 4:13, Ephesians 6:10, Isaiah 41:10

Thought: God doesn't even hear you. Answer: Shut Up Devil, it is written...

That if I Call to Him, He will answer me and show me great and mighty things that I do not know. I know that He hears me and hears me always. It is written that God does not listen to sinners, but if anyone is God-fearing and a worshiper of Him and does His will, He listens to him. Devil, this pertains to me. God's ear is my portion. Since this is my portion, this is the confidence that I have toward him, that if I ask anything according to his will, he hears me. And if I know that he hears me, in whatever I ask, I know that I have the requests that I have asked of him. The Lord is far from the wicked, but he hears the prayer of the righteous. As it is written, the eyes of the Lord are on the righteous, and his ears are open to their prayer. But the face of the Lord is against those who do evil. In Jesus' Name. Amen!

SCRIPTURE REFERENCES

Jeremiah 33:3, John 11:42, john 9:31, 1 John 5:14-15, Proverbs 15:29 1 Peter 3:12

Thought: How do you know that's God's voice. You're going to end up making the wrong decision.
Answer: Shut Up Devil, it is written...

That the path of the righteous is like the morning sun, shining ever brighter till the full light of day. And I have an unction from the Holy One, and I know all things. It is written that the LORD orders the steps of a good man: and he delights in his way. Although I may fall, I shall not be utterly cast down: for the LORD upholds me with his hand. As it is written, the godly may trip seven times, but they will get up again. But one disaster is enough to overthrow the wicked. Devil, you speak as if I'm by myself. As if Christ, the Hope of Glory, does not dwell on the inside of me. He promised not to leave me comfortless. It is written He has given me another Comforter (Counselor, Helper, Intercessor, Advocate, Strengthener, and Standby) and that He may remain with me forever. The Spirit of Truth lives inside me. He will not leave me as an orphan [comfortless, desolate, bereaved, forlorn, helpless]; He will come back for me. In Jesus' Name. Amen!

SCRIPTURE REFERENCES

1 John 2:20, Proverbs 4:18, Psalms 37:23-24 Proverbs 24:16
Colossians 1:27, John 14:16-18,

Thought: You've lost everything, what are you going to do now?
Answer: Shut Up Devil, it is written...

That we walk by faith and not by sight or appearance. It may appear that I've lost everything, but by His Grace, the Blessing is still in my life, and nothing can stop the Blessing. The Blessing will get everything back with abundance and increase, better than it was before. As it is written, The Lord shall increase me more and more, me and my children. This I can expect since I belong to Christ, making me a seed of Abraham and heir according to the promise. I give thanks to the Holy Spirit, my guide and teacher, who speaks to my spirit, bringing me in remembrance of all things He has said. I remember Job, who appeared to have lost everything, but the Blessing was on His life.

Get thee behind me, Satan. Are you so forgetful to how you questioned Job, through His wife saying, "Are you still maintaining your integrity? Curse God and die!" God Forbid!! And Job replied to you by saying, "You are talking like a foolish woman. Shall we accept good from God and not trouble?" In all this, Job did not sin in what he said. And God restored Job. As it is written, the Lord restored the fortunes of Job when he prayed for his friends, and the Lord gave Job twice as much as he had before. If God is for me, who can be against me? And God said he will never leave me, nor forsake me. Now let God be true, and every man a liar. In Jesus' Name. Amen!

SCRIPTURE REFERENCES

John 14:26, 2 Corinthians 5:7, Galatians 3:29,
Psalms 115:14, Job 2:9-10, Job 42:10, Romans 8:31,
Hebrews 13:5, Romans 3:4

Thought: You keep doing good for all these people and they keep abusing you. You might as well stop.
Answer: Shut Up Devil, it is written...

That my love for others will prove to the world that I am His disciple; therefore, I will forgive them, for they know not what they do. And I will not lose heart and grow weary and faint in acting nobly and doing right, for in due time and at the appointed season I shall reap if I do not loosen and relax my courage and faint. It is written, by their fruits you will know them. And faith is only activated, energized, expressed, and works through love. Therefore, I will imitate God in everything I do because I am his dear child. I will live a life filled with love, following the example of Christ. He loved me and offered himself as a sacrifice for me, a pleasing aroma to God. In Jesus' Name. Amen!

SCRIPTURE REFERENCES

John 13:35, Galatians 6:9, Matthew 7:20, Galatians 5:6, Ephesians 5:1-2, Luke 23:34

Thought: That's why your wife/husband/ mother/father/girlfriend/boyfriend/brother/ sister/friend/family/ etc., left you hanging to dry. What are you going to do now? Answer: Shut Up Devil, it is written...

That He will not fail me nor forsake me. My love for others will prove to the world that I am His disciple. So, I'm going to Love! Love is what I'm going to do. For He has left me with exceedingly great and precious promises: that by these, I might partake of the divine nature and escape the corruption that is in the world through lust. It is written that everyone who has given up house or brothers or sisters or mother or father or children or property, for His sake and for the Good News, will receive now in return a hundred times as many houses, brothers, sisters, mothers, children, and property—along with persecution. And in the world to come, that person will have eternal life. His word warns me that it is impossible but that offenses come. And that He has come to set a man against his father, a daughter against her mother, and a daughter-in-law against her mother-in-law. And that my enemies will be right in my own household! But thanks be to God that It is written Blessed *are* those who are persecuted for the sake of righteousness, for theirs is the kingdom of heaven. In Jesus' Name. Amen!

SCRIPTURE REFERENCES

John 13:35, 2 Peter 1:4, Mark 10:29-30, Luke 17:1, Matthew 5:10, Matthew 10:33-36, Joshua 1:5

Thought: Why do You keep giving your hard-earned money to the pastor? Answer: Shut Up Devil, it is written...

That if I give, then [gifts] will be given to me; good measure, pressed down, shaken together, and running over, men shall pour into my bosom. And the measure that I deal out will be measured back to me. It is also written that every good gift and every perfect gift is from above and cometh down from the father of lights. God blessed me with my increase to be a blessing. It is more blessed to give than to receive. It is written, God is not mocked, whatsoever a man sows, that shall He also reap. I will not become weary in doing good, for I will reap a harvest at the proper time if I do not give up. In Jesus' Name. Amen!

SCRIPTURE REFERENCES

Luke 6:38, James 1:17, Act 20:35, Galatians 6:7;9

Thought: Tithing won't help you?
Answer: Shut Up Devil, it is written...

That I shall honor the Lord with my wealth and with the firstfruits and the best part of everything I produce. Only after that will I eat before the Lord my God and rejoice with my entire household. But I will not rob God of what already belongs to Him. Or remove me from under the open window of heaven. As it is written, He will open the windows of heaven, and pour me out a blessing, that there shall not be room enough to receive it. Tithing also rebukes you, Devil. As it is written, He will rebuke the devourer for my sake, and you shall not destroy the fruits of my ground; neither will my vine cast her fruit before the time in the field, saith the LORD of hosts. In Jesus' Name. Amen!

SCRIPTURE REFERENCES

Proverbs 3:9, Malachi 3:8,10,11 Deuteronomy 14:26

Thought: Why do you give to people that don't even appreciate it or care about you?
Answer: Shut Up Devil, it is written...

Obviously, I'm not trying to win the approval of people but of God. If pleasing people were my goal, I would not be Christ's servant. Get thee behind me, Satan. Do you not know that God chose the foolish things of the world to shame the wise, and God chose the weak things of the world to shame the strong? What is more pleasing to the Lord: burnt offerings and sacrifices or obedience to His word. As it is written, obedience is better than sacrifices. I give out of faith, knowing that without faith, it's impossible to please God. Therefore, I give in obedience to His word, knowing that if I give, it shall be given unto me; good measure, pressed down, and shaken together, and running over, shall men give into my bosom. I speak, not to please man, but to please God who tests my heart. In Jesus' Name. Amen!

SCRIPTURE REFERENCES

Galatians 1:10, 1 Corinthians 1:27, 1 Samuel 15:22, Luke 6:38, Hebrews 11:6, 1 Thessalonians 2:4

Thought: You see what's going on, you better save every cent you can.
Answer: Shut Up Devil, it is written...

That the just shall live by faith. The Holy Ghost, who teaches me all things, brings me in remembrance of Issac, who sowed during a famine and received in the same year a hundredfold: and the Lord blessed him. I'm reminded of how he became a very rich man, and his wealth continued to grow. I belong to Christ, which makes me a seed of Abraham and an heir according to the promise. The Lord is my Shepherd to feed, guide, and shield me, and I shall not want or lack for any good thing. As it is written, the lions may grow weak and hungry, but those who seek the LORD lack no good thing. I will bless the Lord, who made an everlasting covenant with me, and forget not all HIS benefits. In Jesus' Name. Amen!

SCRIPTURE REFERENCES

Romans 1:17, John 14:26, Genesis 26:1,12-13, Psalms 23:1, Psalms 34:10, psalms 103:2

Thought: You can't forgive that person for what they did. You're going to look weak. Answer: Shut Up Devil, it is written...

That anyone who believes in him will never be put to shame. As Christ made HIMSELF of no reputation, I will also imitate him and make myself of no reputation. Therefore, I will boast even more gladly in my weaknesses so that Christ's power may rest on me. In my weakness, His strength is indeed made perfect. As it is written, I will be gentle and ready to forgive; not holding grudges and remembering that the Lord first forgave me, so that I might forgive others. I will let love guide my life. They will know I am His disciple by my love. In Jesus' Name. Amen!

SCRIPTURE REFERENCES

Colossians 3:13-14, Romans 10:11, 2 Corinthians 12:9, Philippians 2:7. John 13:35

Thought: You're not happy!
Answer: Shut Up Devil, it is written...

That the joy of the Lord is my strength. Not happiness. Get thee behind me, Satan. Happiness is a temporal emotion subject to change, but joy is a fruit of the spirit, infused with comfort and wrapped in peace with hope in the Lord. Therefore, I will not be dejected or sad. For the God of hope will fill me up with all joy and peace in believing so that by the power of the Holy Spirit, I may abound in hope. I will rejoice in hope, be patient in tribulation, and be constant in prayer. As it is written, my heart is glad, and my whole being rejoices; my flesh also dwells secure. And when the cares of my heart are many, His consolations will cheer my soul. In Jesus' Name. Amen!

SCRIPTURE REFERENCES

Nehemiah 8:10, Romans 15:13, Romans 12:12
psalms 16:9 Psalms 94:19

Thought: You're going to fail!
Answer: Shut Up Devil, it is written...

That He already gives us the victory through our Lord and Savior Jesus Christ. I can't earn the victory. If I could earn the victory, it would be just for the Glory to be mine and not His. I do not work for victory. Get thee behind me, Satan. If you've already been declared victorious in something, you cannot fail at it. Therefore, I enter His rest. As it is written, for only we who believe can enter his rest. As for the others, God said, In my anger, I took an oath: 'They will never enter my place of rest,' although all his works were finished from the foundation of the world. My dependence now is in The Holy Spirit, who lives in me, teaching me all things to bring to past what is already done. So, Christ in me is the Hope of Glory, not me in me. As it is written, I can do all things through Christ, who strengthens me and who always causes me to triumph in Christ. My rest shall remain because His word never tells me to be strong in me and my power, but to be strong in the Lord and the power of his might. In Jesus' Name. Amen!

SCRIPTURE REFERENCES

1 Corinthians 15:57, Romans 8:37, Mark 11:22,
John 14:26, Hebrews 4:3, Colossians 1:27, Philippians 4:13,
2 Corinthians 2:14, Ephesians 6:10.

Thought: Your life doesn't have any meaning?
Answer: Shut Up Devil, it is written...

That I am fearfully and wonderfully made and called according to His purpose. He knows the plans that He has for me, plans of good, and not of evil, to bring me to an expected end. Before He formed me in the womb, He knew and approved of me as His chosen instrument. Before I was born, He separated and set me apart. Shut Up Devil, it is written, Ye have not chosen me, but I have chosen you, and ordained you, that ye should go and bring forth fruit, and that your fruit should remain. Devil, you will not destroy the fruits of my ground; neither shall my vine cast her fruit before the time in the field. In Jesus' Name. Amen!

SCRIPTURE REFERENCES

Jeremiah 29:11, Romans 8:28, Psalms 139:14, Jeremiah 1:5, John 15:16, Malachi 3:11,

Thought: Your children will never be saved. Answer: Shut Up Devil, it is written...

That though they join hand in hand, the wicked shall not go unpunished; but the seed of the righteous shall be delivered. Thanks be to God; Christ has redeemed me from the curse of the law by becoming a curse for me. As it is written, Jesus obtained a more excellent ministry, being the mediator of a better covenant, established upon better promises. Therefore, I'm no longer bound to the law of Moses, which states God will visit the iniquity of the fathers on the children and the children's children, to the third and the fourth generation, but of a better covenant that God is ever mindful of, that states God will increase me more and more, me and my children. As it is written, believe in the Lord Jesus, and you will be saved, along with everyone in my household. Therefore, I wait with patience and a spirit of expectation, knowing that God is faithful to His word and that there shall be a performance of those things which were told. In Jesus' Name. Amen!

SCRIPTURE REFERENCES

Proverbs 11:21, Galatians 3:13, Hebrews 8:6, Exodus 34:7, psalms 111:5, Acts 16:31, Luke 1:45

Thought: You think you know everything. Answer: Shut Up Devil, it is written...

That I have an unction from the Holy One, and I know all things because greater is He that is in me, than He that is in the world. We tell others about Christ, warning everyone and teaching everyone with all the wisdom God has given us. Christ in us is the Hope of Glory. As it is written, for the LORD giveth wisdom: out of His mouth cometh knowledge and understanding, and He lays up sound wisdom for the righteous. Yet I speak wisdom among those who are mature, not the wisdom of this world, nor of the rulers of this world, who will come to nothing. I receive the wisdom that the Lord has given me. And I receive it by faith. In Jesus' Name. Amen!

SCRIPTURE REFERENCES

1 John 2:20, 1 John 4:4, Colossians 1:27-28,
Proverbs 2:6-7, 1 Corinthians 2:6

Thought: Aren't you tired of making excuses for God when HE doesn't deliver? Answer: Shut Up Devil, it is written...

That He is God alone. There are many plans in the mind of a man, but it is the purpose of the Lord that will stand. Thanks be to God that we are called according to His purpose. As it is written, all things work together for good, for those who are called according to His purpose. God does not need me to uphold His reputation. Nor will I be humiliated or ashamed. As it is written, Do not be afraid; you will not be put to shame. Do not fear disgrace; you will not be humiliated. You will forget the shame of your youth. I know the Lord watches over those who do right, and His ears are open to their prayers. Shut up, Devil. I know that God chose the foolish things of the world to shame the wise, and God chose the weak things of the world to shame the strong. So, it may appear through the senses that you're winning and making excuses for my losses, but the truth is God always causes me to triumph in Christ, and the works were finished before the foundation of the world. As it is written, we who have believed enter that rest. In Jesus' Name. Amen!

SCRIPTURE REFERENCES

Psalms 86:10, Proverbs 19:21, Romans 8:28, Isaiah 54:4, 1 Peter 3:12, 1 Corinthians 1:27, Hebrews 4:3

Thought: You don't have any favor of God in your life. You are just like everyone else. If you had a favor, why aren't you getting what you want?
Answer: Shut Up Devil, it is written...

That the just shall live by faith. It is also written for me not to be anxious about anything, but in every situation, by prayer and petition, with thanksgiving, to present my requests to God. In doing this, the peace of God, which surpasses all understanding, will guard my heart and my mind in Christ Jesus. I could never be like anyone else. God does not make duplicates. He made all the delicate inner parts of my body and knitted me together in my mother's womb. I am fearfully and wonderfully made. Of this, I know! As it is written, I increase in wisdom, stature, and favor with God and man every day. The favor of God surrounds me as with a shield. The things you speak of are already done. Just like you are already defeated. My heart's eye sees it clearly. My Spirit bears witness to this truth. As it is written, there are three that bear record in heaven, the Father, the Word, and the Holy Ghost: these three are one. Besides, if I faint in the day of adversity, my strength is proven small, but if I don't faint, in due season, I shall reap. In Jesus' Name. Amen!

SCRIPTURE REFERENCES

Philippians 4:7-8, Romans 1:17, Psalms 139:13-14, Luke 2:52, Psalms 5:12, 1 John 5:7, Proverbs 24:10, Galatians 6:9

Thought: You're not going to get through this?
Answer: Shut Up Devil, it is written...

That I can do all things through Christ who strengthens me, and I will be strong in the Lord and the power of His might. My faith is in the greater one who dwells in me. My faith is not in myself. As it is written, have faith in God, and undoubtedly greater is He who is in me than the He that is in the world. It is finished! Jesus got the victory, and I'm in Christ. As it is written, thanks be to God, who gives us the victory through our Lord Jesus Christ. Therefore, I already got through this as His works were done before the foundation of the world. He is the author and finisher of my faith who calls the end from the beginning. My soul can rest in Him who is gentle and lowly in the heart because He knows the way that I take; and when he has tried me, I shall come forth as pure as gold. In Jesus' Name. Amen!

SCRIPTURE REFERENCES

Philippians 4:13, Ephesians 6:10, Mark 11:22, 1 John 4:4, Job 23:10, John 19:30, 1 Corinthians 15:57, John 17:24, Hebrews 12:2, Isaiah 46:10, Matthew 11:29

Thought: You're lazy?
Answer: Shut Up Devil, it is written...

For me to be anxious for nothing, I am taking no thought for my life or whether I have enough food and drink or enough clothes to wear. I'm put in remembrance of Mary, who sat at Jesus feet as he taught, while Martha was cumbered about much serving. I, like Mary, will choose the one thing worth being concerned about: the good part that will never be taken from me. That is to remain at the feet of Jesus and cling to every word that proceeds out of the mouth of God (His Word). I will wait on the Lord and be of good courage, knowing that He shall strengthen my heart. You are a thief and a master deceiver. My loving Father will advise me with a gentle nudge if I am slothful as He is meek and lowly in heart. But I take no counsel from a roaring Lion with a mouth full of false truths, deceit, and lies. As it is written, you are a liar and the father of it. In Jesus' Name. Amen!

SCRIPTURE REFERENCES

Philippians 4:6, Matthew 6:25, Luke 10:39-42,
Psalms 27:14, John 10:10, Daniel 8:25, John 8:44,
Matthew 11:29, 1 Peter 5:8.

Thought: If you're so righteous, then why do you keep sinning?
Answer: Shut Up Devil, it is written...

That my righteousness is a gift that I received through the abundant provision of God's Grace, and I reign through the one man Jesus Christ. My righteousness cannot be earned by my works as it is written, not by works, so that no one can boast. So that, no flesh should glory in his presence. All of us have become like one who is unclean, and all our righteous acts are like filthy rags; we all shrivel up like a leaf, and like the wind, our sins sweep us away. For all have sinned and come short of the glory of God. But thanks be to God; I stand as a redeemed child of the highest God under no condemnation. Because there is now no condemnation to them which are in Christ Jesus, who walk not after the flesh, but after the Spirit. As it is written, I have swept away your offenses like a cloud, your sins like the morning mist. Return to me, for I have redeemed you. So, I return to Him as I must, no longer burdened to the yoke of slavery but freed in Christ Jesus. And whom the Son sets free, is free indeed. Jesus is my burnt offering and final offering forevermore. In Jesus' Name. Amen!

SCRIPTURE REFERENCES

Romans 5:17, 1 Corinthians 1:29, Ephesians 2:9, Isaiah 64:6, Romans 3:23, Isaiah 44:22, Galatians 5:1, John 8:36

Thought: You're going to be overtaken by all your problems.
Answer: Shut Up Devil, it is written...

That He will not suffer my foot to be moved, my God will keep me, and neither slumbers nor sleeps. I shall always keep my eyes on the Lord because I know that I will not be shaken with him at my right hand. I am of a Kingdom that cannot be moved. He will keep me in perfect peace because my mind stays on Him. I trust Him. Therefore, I will not be afraid or discouraged because of this vast army of problems because the battle is not mine but God's. Since the battle is not mine, I will give all my worries and cares to God because He cares about me. In Jesus' Name. Amen!

SCRIPTURE REFERENCES

Psalms 16:8, Isaiah 26:3, Hebrews 12:28, 2 Chronicles 20:15, 1 Peter 5:7, Psalms 121:3

Thought: Your enemy fell, I guess you can be happy now.
Answer: Shut Up Devil, it is written...

For me not to rejoice when my enemies fall or to be happy when they stumble. If I do, the Lord will be displeased with me and turn His anger away from them. You're a liar! You're my ONLY enemy, the ancient serpent called the Devil, who deceives the whole world. You are the master of deception and the father of lies. There is no truth in you, and you speak your native language. But thanks be to God; your schemes have not outwitted me. You are a thief! As it is written, the thief's purpose is to steal, kill, and destroy. But thanks be to God; the thief has been caught today! And if the thief is found, it is written that he must pay back sevenfold; he must give up all the wealth of his house. In Jesus' Name. Amen!

SCRIPTURE REFERENCES

Proverbs 24:17-18, Revelation 12:9, Daniel 8:25, John 8:44, 2 Corinthians 2:11, John 10:10, Proverbs 6:31

Thought: After all they did to you, you deserve to hate them.
Answer: Shut Up Devil, it is written...

For me to love others, as Jesus has loved me. How can I say I love God, whom I haven't seen, yet hate my brother, whom I see every day? Since I love God, I must love my brother also. As it is written, everyone who hates his brother is a murderer. I will remain in love and stay in his love. As it is written, the only thing that counts is faith expressing itself through love. I will be merciful, just as my father is merciful. As it is written, Do not judge, and you will not be judged. Do not condemn, and you will not be condemned. Forgive, and you will be forgiven. I am forgiven, and I rest in the finished work of my forgiveness. In Jesus' Name. Amen!

SCRIPTURE REFERENCES

John 15:10;12-13, 1 John 4:20-21, 1 John 3:15, Galatians 5:6, Luke 6:36-37, Hebrews 4:10.

Thought: After all they did to you, you deserve to be angry and bitter. They don't deserve your forgiveness. Answer: Shut Up Devil, it is written...

For me to let all bitterness, wrath, anger, clamor, slander, and all malice be put away, but instead be kind and tenderhearted, forgiving one another, just as God through Christ has forgiven me. I will not fail to obtain the Grace of God and allow a root of bitterness to spring up and cause many others to be defiled. Get behind me, Satan. Although I'm angry, I will not sin and give you any foothold or opportunity to work in my life. I, myself, did not deserve forgiveness, but God showed His great love for me by sending Christ to die for me while I was still sinning. Just as my father forgave me, I choose to forgive also. As it is written, to make allowance for each other's faults and forgive anyone who offends me. So that I can forgive others. In Jesus' Name. Amen!

SCRIPTURE REFERENCES

Ephesians 4:31-32, Hebrews 12:15, Ephesians 4:26-27, Romans 5:8, Colossians 3:13-14.

Thought: They deserve to be punished and ashamed after what they did. Answer: Shut Up Devil, it is written...

That whatever I am now, it is all because God poured out His special favor on me. But for the Grace of God, I am what I am. I, too, deserve to be punished. I will not think of myself more highly than I ought to think. Although I am angry, it is written, to never avenge myself, but to leave it to the wrath of God. As it is written, "Vengeance is mine, I will repay, says the Lord." God dispenses His vengeance in proportion as He ONLY sees fit. But I know He will avenge me speedily. God has not destined my posture for wrath but to obtain salvation through our Lord Jesus Christ, who died for me so that whether I'm awake or asleep, I might live with him. But if He blotted out my sins and covered my shame. Is God a respecter of person that, if they come to repentance, He will not restore them and cover their shame too? Of course, He will. In that, my Father wants me to bless them than curse me and do good to them than hate me. As it is written, if your enemies are hungry, give them food to eat. If they are thirsty, give them water to drink. In doing this, I will heap burning coals of shame on their heads, and the Lord will reward me. In Jesus' Name. Amen!

SCRIPTURE REFERENCES

1 Corinthian 15:10, Romans 12:3;19,
1 Thessalonians 5;9-10, Luke 18:8, Proverbs 25:21-22,
Isaiah 44:22, Acts 10:34, Luke 6:27-28

Thought: Just Give Up!
Answer: Shut Up Devil, it is written...

For me not to grow weary in well-doing, in due season I will reap if I do not give up. I know my breakthrough is coming. Therefore, I will take courage and not let my hands be weak, knowing that my work shall be rewarded. I will rejoice in hope, being patient in tribulation, and be constant in prayer, knowing Great is His faithfulness and that He will avenge me speedily. Get thee behind me, Satan! You speak as if the Lord is standing afar off or hiding in my times of trouble. God Forbid! He is an ever-present help in times of trouble. The Evil has the task of gathering up the harvest to dispense to the righteous. As it is written, for the person who pleases Him, God gives wisdom, knowledge, and joy; but to the sinner, He gives the work of gathering and collecting so that He may give to the one who pleases God. Surely God will break the arms of the wicked evil people until the last one is destroyed. Therefore, I wait with expectancy that Instead of my shame, I will receive a double portion, and instead of disgrace, I will rejoice in my inheritance. And I will inherit a double portion in my land, and everlasting joy will be mine. In Jesus' Name. Amen!

SCRIPTURE REFERENCES

Galatians 6:9, 2 Chronicles 15:7, Romans 12:12, Lamentations 3:23, Luke 18:8, Psalms 10:15, Matthew 16:23, Isaiah 61:7, Ecclesiastes 2:26, Psalms 46:1

Thought: Aren't you mad because everybody else around you is getting blessed? They're not even living right. Answer: Shut Up Devil, it is written...

That He is the Lord, and there is no one else; there is no God except Him. Our God is in heaven, and He does whatever pleases Him. As it is written, Whatever the Lord pleases, He does, in heaven and on earth, in the seas and all deeps. What shall I say then? Is God unjust? Not at all! He will have mercy on whom He chooses to have mercy, and He will have compassion on whom He chooses to have compassion. Nevertheless, get thee behind me, Satan, for I am blessed in the city and blessed in the field. I am in everlasting covenant with my Heavenly Father. As it is written, I will establish my covenant as an everlasting covenant between you and me and your descendants after you for the generations to come, to be your God and the God of your descendants after you. And God is ever mindful of his covenant. Since I belong to Christ, then I am Abraham's seed and heirs according to the promise. I'm already blessed. Therefore, I will please my neighbor for His good, to build him up and rejoice when He rejoices-not looking to my interests, but also to the interests of others. I will not grow weary in well-doing; in due season, I will reap if I do not give up. In Jesus' Name. Amen!

SCRIPTURE REFERENCES

Isaiah 45:5, Romans 9:14-15, Psalms 115:3, Psalms 135:6, Matthew 16:23, Deuteronomy 28:3, Genesis 17:7, Psalms 111:5, Galatians 3:29, Romans 15:2, Philippians 2:4, Galatians 6:9

Thought: You're always screwing up. Answer: Shut Up Devil, it is written...

That you are a liar and there is no truth in you. You've been a liar from the beginning. I am certain that God, who began the good work within me, will continue his work until it is finished on the day when Christ Jesus returns. I will fix my eyes on Jesus, who is the pioneer and perfecter of my faith because we are all infected and impure with sin, and when we display our righteous deeds, they're nothing but filthy rags. Therefore, I will not rely on my works as righteousness. But rather rejoice in the truth that He made me righteous. As it is written, since we have been made righteous through his faithfulness combined with our faith, we have peace with God through our Lord Jesus Christ. So, I rest in the finished works of Jesus; that no flesh should glory in His presence. Therefore, I will boast even more gladly about my weaknesses so that Christ's power may rest on me. In Jesus' Name. Amen!

SCRIPTURE REFERENCES

Hebrews 12:2, Philippians 1:6, John 8:44, Isaiah 64:6, Romans 5:1, 1 Corinthians 1:29, 2 Corinthians 12:9

Thought: You broke your promise to God, and He is angry with you.
Answer: Shut Up Devil, it is written...

That if I confess my sins, He is faithful and just and will forgive me of my sins and cleanse me from all unrighteousness. Jesus was the one who was found without fault. Therefore, I rest in the finished works of what Christ has done. As it is written, God made Him who had no sin to be sin for me, so that in him, I might become the righteousness of God. I will grow in truth and become mature in the faith not to make rash promises to my Heavenly Father, who is seated in heaven. As it is written, not to make rash promises and not to be hasty in bringing matters before God. After all, God is in heaven, and I am here on earth. So, I will let my words be few. Get behind me, Satan. I am in Christ, and there is no condemnation to them which are in Christ Jesus, who walk not after the flesh but after the Spirit. I have an everlasting covenant with God that He will never be angry with me or punish me. As it is written, so now I swear that I will never again be angry and punish you. In Jesus' Name. Amen!

SCRIPTURE REFERENCES

1 John 1:9, 2 Corinthians 5:21, Ephesians 4:15, Ecclesiastes 5:2, Romans 8:1, Isaiah 54:9

Thought: There's no hope!
Answer: Shut Up Devil, it is written...

That God is hope. As it is written, may the God of hope fill us with all joy and peace in believing so that by the power of the Holy Spirit, we may abound in hope. Therefore, I rejoice in hope. My faith is activated in hope. As it is written, faith is the evidence of things hoped for. It is by hope that I was saved. Hope that is seen is not hope. As it is written, for who hopes for what he sees? But if we hope for what we do not see, we wait for it with patience. Therefore, the scriptures were written. They were written for our instruction, that we might have hope through endurance and the encouragement of the Scriptures. In Jesus' Name. Amen!

SCRIPTURE REFERENCES

Romans 15:13, Romans 12:12, Hebrews 11:1,
Romans 8:24-25, Romans 15:4

Thought: You're going to die!
Answer: Shut Up Devil, it is written...

That I shall not die, but live, and declare the works of the Lord. It is with long life He will satisfy me and show me His salvation. For I am in Christ, and everyone who lives in Him and believes in Him will never die. All souls are His. Therefore, I will not fear those who kill the body but cannot kill the soul. I rejoice in that He will not abandon my soul to Hades or let me see corruption. My life is redeemed from destruction. As it is written, He redeems my life from destruction and crowns me with lovingkindness and tender mercies. He also satisfies my mouth with good things so that my youth is renewed like the eagle. In Jesus' Name. Amen!

SCRIPTURE REFERENCES

Psalms 118:17, John 11:26, Ezekiel 18:4, Matthew 10:28, Acts 2:27, psalms 91:16, Psalms 103:4-6

Thought: You'll never find a spouse. Answer: Shut Up Devil, it is written...

That a man who isolates himself seeks his desires, and he rages against all wise judgment, but I desire a partner. My Heavenly Father said that it is not good for man to be alone and that He will make a helper suitable for me. As it is written, one can chase a thousand, but two can put ten thousand to flight. As it is written, a man shall leave his father and his mother and hold fast to his wife, and they shall become one flesh. Get thee behind me, Satan; the Lord knows my desires. Not that I'm in need because I've learned to be content whatever the circumstances, but it is He who gave me the desire. And as I delight myself in Him, He will continue to give me the desires of my heart. As it is written, whatever you ask for in prayer, believe that you have received it, and it will be yours. Therefore, it is already done. My spouse has been signed, sealed, and delivered according to the word of God. And His word is forever settled in heaven. He will supply my every need, according to His riches in glory in Christ Jesus. I am favored by the Lord. As it is written, He who finds a wife finds a good thing and obtains favor from the Lord. In Jesus' Name. Amen!

SCRIPTURE REFERENCES

Genesis 2:18, Proverbs 18:1, Genesis 2:24, Philippians 4:19, Psalms 37:4, Proverbs 18:22 Mark 11:24, Deuteronomy 32:30

Thought: No reason to give Him praise right now.
Answer: Shut Up Devil, it is written...

That in everything, to give thanks. My praise is not contingent upon my circumstance or situation. Get behind me, Satan. I am to praise continually, offering up a sacrifice of praise to my God. It is the fruit of my lips that acknowledges His name. I will forever give Him praise. I will Praise Him in his sanctuary; I will praise Him in his mighty heavens! I will Praise Him for his mighty deeds; I will praise Him according to his excellent greatness. Lest the rocks cry out in my place. God Forbid. God is spirit, and those who worship Him must worship in spirit and truth. He is always worthy of my praise. Therefore, I will exalt Him, for He rescued me. He refused to let my enemy triumph over me. I cried to Him for help, and He restored my health. Weeping may last through the night, but joy comes with the morning. As it is written, He has appointed unto them that mourn in Zion, beauty for ashes, the oil of joy for mourning, and the garment of praise for the spirit of heaviness; that they might be called trees of righteousness, the planting of the Lord, that He might be glorified. Therefore, I have a spirit of expectancy for His everlasting covenant to be fulfilled. For my shame, I will have double; and for confusion, I shall rejoice in my portion: everlasting joy shall be mine. In Jesus' Name. Amen!

SCRIPTURE REFERENCES

Hebrews 13:15, 1 Thessalonians 5:18, Luke 19:40, John 4:24, Psalms 150:1-2, psalms 30:1, Isaiah 61:3;7

Thought: You can't have kids. You are barren. Answer: Shut Up Devil, it is written...

That the fruit of my womb is blessed, I will look unto Abraham, my father, and unto Sarah that bore me: Whom God has an everlasting covenant with. As it is written, I will establish an everlasting covenant between you and me and your descendants after you for the generations to come, to be your God and the God of your descendants after you. Get behind me, Satan! I belong to Christ, making me a seed of Abraham and heir according to the promise. Therefore, instead of sorrow, I will rejoice and praise God in knowing the truth. The truth is he gives the barren woman a home, making her the joyous mother of children. Because the days are coming when they will say, 'Blessed are the barren and the wombs that never bore and the breasts that never nursed!' As it is written, Isaac prayed to the Lord for His wife to bear a child, and He granted Him his request. Therefore, He will also grant my request since He is not a respecter of persons. I shall surely conceive. Just as Rebekah conceived, I will conceive. I receive this by Faith with a blessed assurance within my heart that this is the will of my Lord. As it is written, children are a heritage from the Lord, and the fruit of the womb is a reward, and like arrows in the hand of a warrior are the children of one's youth. In Jesus' Name. Amen!

SCRIPTURE REFERENCES

Isaiah 51:1, Genesis 17:7, Psalms 113:9, Luke 23:29,
Galatians 3:29, Genesis 25:21, Deuteronomy 28:4,
1 John 3:19, Psalms 127:3,4

Thought: You're just a lost soul. Answer: Shut Up Devil, it is written...

That, therefore, the son of man came to seek and to save the lost. I'm grateful to the King of Glory to proclaim that I was once lost, but now I'm found. I was once blind, but now I see. As it is written, I did not choose Him, but He chose me and ordained me that I might go and bring forth fruit and that my fruit should remain. Now that my Heavenly Father has chosen me, no one shall pluck me out of His hand. And I am convinced that nothing shall separate me from His love. Get behind me, Satan! How dare you accuse me whom God has chosen for his own? No one, for God himself, has given me the right standing with himself. I can never be lost when my daddy knows where I am. And He will command his angels concerning me to guard me in all my ways. His word is a lamp unto my feet and a light unto my path. And I am cleaned through His word, which He has spoken unto me. That if I abide in Him, and He in him, that I will bring forth much fruit; knowing that without Him, I can do nothing. In Jesus' Name. Amen!

SCRIPTURE REFERENCES

Luke 19:10, Luke 15:24, John 15:16, John 10:28, Romans 8:33;38, Psalms 91:11, Psalms 119:105, John 15:3-5

Thought: Where are your friends now? Answer: Shut Up Devil, it is written...

That even when my father and my mother forsake me, the Lord will receive me. He will never leave me nor forsake me. Therefore, my soul waits silently for God alone; He alone is my expectation. As it is written, cursed is the one who trusts in man, who draws strength from mere flesh, and whose heart turns away from the Lord. But blessed is the one who trusts in the Lord, whose confidence is in Him. Therefore, my trust is in Him, and He will keep me in perfect peace. Friends are not my hope and not the way. God is my only hope, and Jesus is the only way. As it is written, I am the way, the truth, and the life. His grace is all I need. His grace is more than sufficient. I choose to forgive my friends, and I will not be hot-tempered and store up conflict. Instead, I will let love and loyalty show like a necklace and write it on my mind. Always! In Jesus' Name. Amen!

SCRIPTURE REFERENCES

Psalms 27:10, Deuteronomy 31:6, Psalms 62:5, Jeremiah 17:5;7, Isaiah 26:3, John 14:6, Psalms 39:7, Proverbs 3:3, 2 Corinthians 12:9, proverbs 15:18

Thought: Nobody Cares!
Answer: Shut Up Devil, it is written...

That we do not have a high priest, who cannot be touched with the feeling of our infirmities, He knows how I'm feeling, and He cares. The thief comes to steal, kill, and destroy. You can't steal my joy. I will not bite the seed of victimization. I am not a victim; I am victorious. It is the Lord who goes with me to fight for me against my enemies to give me victory. He trains my hands for war and my fingers for battle. God has also blessed me with resources, brothers, and sisters in the faith to encourage me and lift me up in times of sorrow and tribulation. He has also blessed me with His angels, ministering Spirits, who minister for me as an heir of salvation. They excel in strength and do His commandments, hearkening to the voice of His word. They all intercede for me. It is also Christ, who is even at the right hand of God, who also makes intercession for me. Get behind me, Satan. Even the lions may grow weak and hungry, but those who seek the Lord lack no good thing. My joy comes from the Lord. As it is written, in His presence, there is a fulness of joy. In Jesus' Name. Amen!

SCRIPTURE REFERENCES

John 10:10, Deuteronomy 20:4, psalms 16:11, Romans 8:34, Hebrews 1:14, Psalms 34:10, Psalms 144:1, Hebrews 4:15

Thought: Why are you thanking JESUS in the middle of your storm?
Answer: Shut Up Devil, it is written...

That my trouble will not always last, as it is written, the suffering won't last forever. It won't be long before this generous God who has great plans for me in Christ - eternal and glorious plans they are! Will have me put together and on my feet for good. Therefore, I count it all joy when I encounter trials of many kinds because I know that the testing of my faith develops perseverance. And I will allow perseverance to finish its work so that I may be mature and complete, not lacking anything. My government does not operate like the world's government. I will not forsake the mysteries of the kingdom of heaven. As it is written, it is given unto me to know the mysteries of the kingdom of heaven, but to them, it is not given. Therefore, I will not be anxious about anything, but in everything, by prayer and supplication with thanksgiving, I will let my requests be made known unto God. Thanksgiving is the will of God for my life. As it is written, give thanks in all circumstances, for this is the will of God in Christ Jesus for you. I give thanks to the Lord because He is good, for his steadfast love endures forever! I give thanks because I am the redeemed. As it is written, let the redeemed of the Lord tell their story. I will give thanks to the Lord for his unfailing love and his wonderful deeds for humankind. For It is He who satisfies my thirst and fills my hunger with good things. In Jesus' Name. Amen!

SCRIPTURE REFERENCES

James 1:2-4, Matthew 13:11, Philippians 4:6,
1 Thessalonians 5:18, Psalms 107:1-2;8-9, 1 Peter 5:10

Thought: See, you lost!
Answer: Shut Up Devil, it is written...

That we walk by faith (what God said) and not by sight (the sense realm), it is written that the just shall live by faith. Because I know that it may look, with the natural eye, as if I lost, but me losing is not the word spoken over my life by the Father of lights. For God said that He always causes me to triumph in Christ, and He uses me to spread the aroma of the knowledge of Him everywhere I go. I am, to God, the pleasing aroma of Christ among those who are being saved and those who are perishing. There is no losing in the Kingdom of God, for this government is an ever-increasing government, an unshakable government. As it is written, I have received an unshakeable Kingdom; therefore, I will be thankful and please God by worshiping Him with holy fear and awe-knowing that my God is a consuming fire. Get under my feet, Devil. You shall trample under my feet forever. As it is written, you will trample upon lions and cobras; you will crush fierce lions and serpents under your feet! This immovable, unshakable, ever-increasing government is upon the shoulders of my savior, Jesus the Christ. As it is written, a child is born, unto us, a son is given, and the government shall be upon his shoulders: and His name shall be called Wonderful, Counselor, The mighty God, The everlasting Father, The Prince of Peace. Of the increase of His government and peace, there shall be no end, upon the throne of David, and upon His kingdom, to order it, and to establish it with judgment and with justice from henceforth even forever. And the zeal of the Lord of hosts will perform this. In Jesus' Name. Amen!

SCRIPTURE REFERENCES

2 Corinthians 5:7, Romans 1:17, 2 Corinthians 2:14-15, Isaiah 9:6, Hebrews 12:28-29, Psalms 91:13

Thought: You can't stop sinning. Sin is too powerful.
Answer: Shut Up Devil, it is written...

That I have died to the law through the body of Christ, so that I may belong to another. The power of sin is in the law. I now serve the newness of spirit and not the oldness of the letter. Jesus is my sin offering once and for all. He nailed it all to the cross. As it is written, He forgave us all our sins and canceled the charge of my legal indebtedness, which stood against me and condemned me; he has taken it away, nailing it to the cross. For my sake, he made Jesus be sin, who knew no sin so that in Him I might become the righteousness of God. There is, therefore, now no condemnation for those who are in Christ Jesus. Because of this truth and because I am a new creature in Christ, I can now come boldly before the throne of grace. Get behind me, Devil. My savior spoiled your house and stripped all your power and authority that the wages of sin caused, which was death. In Jesus' Name. Amen!

SCRIPTURE REFERENCES

Colossians 2:13-14, Romans 7:4;6, 2 Corinthians 5:21, Romans 8:1, Hebrews 4:16

Thought: If you're so blessed, why don't you have any evidence?
Answer: Shut Up Devil, it is written...

That surely the Lord blesses the righteous; He surrounds them with His favor as with a shield. Get behind me, Satan. The evidence of the blessing saturates me. In all circumstances, I will give thanks. I will have a heart of gratitude for the things the wicked take for granted. The sight of my children is evidence of the blessing. As it is written, children are a blessing and a gift from the Lord. I go to sleep each night, trusting in the Lord, and the fact that I woke up this morning to new mercies is a blessing. As it is written, the steadfast love of the Lord never ceases; His mercies never come to an end; they are new every morning. The truth that He did not leave me comfortless is a blessing, but He left me with His precious Holy Spirit to strengthen me, intercede for me, counsel me, guide me, to show me things to come, to teach me all things, and bring me in remembrance of the things He said to me. What is man, that He is mindful of me? To think that a perfect, blameless, and Holy God would dwell in this earthen vessel causes my soul to rejoice and cry out HALLELUJAH. I know that good itself does not dwell in me, that is, in my sinful nature. For I have the desire to do what is good, but I cannot carry it out. But it is Christ in me who is the Hope of Glory. This is the mystery that has been hidden for ages but now is made manifest in His Saints. As it is written, greater is He that is in me than He that is in the world. This is more evidence of the blessing. And my soul knows it right well. In Jesus' Name. Amen!

SCRIPTURE REFERENCES

Psalms 5:12, 1 Thessalonians 5:18, Psalms 127:3, Lamentations 3:22-23. Psalms 143:8, John 14:26, Psalms 8:4, Luke 1:46-47, Romans 7:18, Colossians 1:26-27, 1 John 4:4, Psalms 139:14

Thought: The wicked have more evidence of the blessing than you do.
Answer: Shut Up Devil, it is written...

That He causes His sun to rise on the evil and the good and sends rain on the righteous and the unrighteous. But God is good to all. But If I cherished sin in my heart, the Lord would not listen; but God has surely listened and has heard my prayer. Therefore, I praise my God, who has not rejected my prayer or withheld his love from me! The prosperity of the wicked awaits the evil day of sorrow, but my blessing comes with no sorrow. As it is written, the blessing of the Lord makes rich, and He adds no sorrow with it. Get behind me, Satan. You are the old serpent who deceived the whole world. To the person who pleases God, He gives wisdom, knowledge, and happiness, but to the sinner, He gives the task of gathering and storing up wealth to hand it over to the one who pleases God. As it is written, the sinner's wealth is laid up for the righteous. Therefore, I will never envy the wicked. Soon they fade away like grass and disappear. But instead, I will trust in the Lord. In Jesus' Name. Amen!

SCRIPTURE REFERENCES

Matthew 5:45, Psalms 66:18-20, proverbs 10:22, Psalms 37:1-3, Ecclesiastes 2:26, Proverbs 13:22

Thought: You don't even feel close to God right now.
Answer: Shut Up Devil, it is written...

That the just shall live by faith, not by feeling! Faith in what? Faith in His word! Get behind me, Satan. Man shall not live by bread alone but by every word that proceeds out the mouth of God, for He is the word. As it is written, In the beginning, was the word, and the word was with God, and the Word was God. He knows where I am and the path that I take. He knows how I feel. For we have not a high priest which cannot be touched with the feeling of our infirmities. He is *El Roi*. The God who sees me, for He is close to the brokenhearted and saves those who are crushed in spirit. Therefore, I will wait on the Lord; and be of good courage, knowing that He will strengthen my heart. I probably would have fainted unless I believed that I would see the goodness of the Lord in the land of the living. I have a friend in Jesus and sonship with my Heavenly Father. As it is written, I no longer call your servants because a servant doesn't know his master's business. Instead, I have called your friends. Therefore, I cling to His word that He will never leave me nor forsake me. My feelings do not triumph over His word. His word is forever settled in heaven. His compassions fail not! But they are new every morning. When my faithfulness runs out, I remember great is His faithfulness. The Lord is forever my portion. And My soul says YES. Therefore, I hope in him. In Jesus' Name. Amen!

SCRIPTURE REFERENCES

Romans 1:17, Matthew 4:4, John 1:1, Psalms 34:18
Lamentation 3:22-24, Psalms 27:13-14, John 15:15,
Psalms 119:89, Hebrews 4:15, Deuteronomy 31:6

Thought: You Sinned!
You missed the mark.
Answer: Shut Up Devil, it is written...

That if I confess my sins, He is faithful and just to forgive me of my sins and to cleanse me from all unrighteousness. I am justified freely by His grace through the redemption that is in Jesus Christ. All have sinned and come short of the Glory of God. Therefore, I will not allow your perverted guilt and shame to rob me of the joy that remains on the inside of me from this truth. But rather remind you that I do not depend on my righteousness. As it is written, we are all unclean, and all our righteousness are as filthy rags. Therefore, I cling to the gift of righteousness, where the abundance of grace shall reign through the life of one, Jesus Christ. My branch abides in Him, the true vine. My joy remains intact, and my joy remains full because I know it's not of my righteousness but the righteousness of Jesus Christ, the rock on which I stand. He has changed my shame into praise. Whoever believes in Him will never be put to shame. As it is written, The Lord will rescue his servants; no one who takes refuge in him will be condemned. In Jesus' Name. Amen!

SCRIPTURE REFERENCES

Romans 3:23-24, Isaiah 64:6, Romans 5:17, John 15:5;11, 1 John 1:9, Zephaniah 3:19, Romans 10:11, Psalms 34:22

Thought: You lost yourself in Christ. Answer: Shut Up Devil, it is written...

That He will not allow my foot to be moved, He will not slumber as He keeps watch over me. It is He who keeps my feet. He will keep the feet of His Saints. By strength shall no man prevail. As it is written, my sheep listen to my voice; I know them, and they follow me. I give them eternal life, and they shall never perish; no one will pluck them out of my hand. Get behind me, Devil! You cannot condemn me. There is, therefore, now no condemnation to them which are in Christ Jesus. As it is written, Who shall bring any charge against God's elect; when it is God himself who justifies me. Who shall come forward and accuse or impeach those whom God has chosen for himself? Who is there to condemn me? Every word of God proves true. He is a shield to all who come to him for protection. My soul waits only upon God, for my expectation is only from him. He alone is my rock and my salvation: He is my defense; I shall not be moved. In Jesus' Name. Amen!

SCRIPTURE REFERENCES

Psalms 121:3, John 10:27-28, Proverbs 30:4, Romans 8:1, Romans 8:33-34, 1 Samuel 2:9, Psalms 62:5-6

Thought: You need to tone down your passion for Christ. It's too overbearing for people!
Answer: Shut Up Devil, it is written...

That I am not ashamed of the gospel because it is the power of God that brings salvation to everyone who believes. I will not choke the anointing through unbelief and perish by following their example of disobedience. Get behind me, Satan! God forbid that I agree. As it is written, If I say, I will not make mention of the Lord or speak any more in His name, in my mind and heart it is as if there were a burning fire shut up in my bones. And I will not quench the Holy Spirit. Instead, I will be like the voice of one crying out in the wilderness saying make straight the way of the Lord. And I know that those who went out from us did not truly belong to us. For if they had belonged to us, they would have remained with us. In Jesus' Name. Amen!

SCRIPTURE REFERENCES

Romans 1:16, Jeremiah 20:9-10, Hebrews 4:11,
1 Thessalonians 5:19, Isaiah 40:3, 1 John 2:19

Thought: Just do it! You know you want to.
Answer: Shut Up Devil, it is written...

That without faith, it is impossible to please God and that those who are in the flesh cannot please Him. I shut the mouth of my screaming flesh with a strict denial. And yield to the Spirit that speaks to my inner man. The real me! Get behind me, Satan! You are a liar; you've been one from the beginning, and you are beneath my feet! I crucify my flesh of its passions and desires daily because I belong to Christ. And if I belong to Christ, I am also crucified with Christ. Nevertheless, I live, yet not I, but Christ lives in me. And the life I now live, I live by faith in the Son of God. It's available to me, so I receive more grace by faith to discipline my body and bring it into subjection. My Heavenly Father owns my body. It has been presented as a living sacrifice. It is holy and acceptable unto God. It is my reasonable service to him. Considering all he has done for me. In Jesus' Name. Amen!

SCRIPTURE REFERENCES

Romans 8:8, Hebrews 11:6, Galatians 2:20, Galatians 5:24, 1 Corinthians 9:27, Romans 12:2

Thought: Just Accept Defeat! It's not a big deal. You can't win them all. Answer: Shut Up Devil, it is written...

That I've been made unto God a King and priest on the earth and will reign on the earth, and where the word of a King is, there is power. I win every battle! I don't win a few; I don't lose a few. But I win every battle. As it is written, thanks be unto God, who always causes me to triumph in Christ. Not sometimes, but always causes me to triumph. Not win a few, lose a few, but always! Get behind me, Satan. It is written that I am more than a conqueror through Him who loved me. Therefore, I win every battle! Because I am the righteousness of God through Christ Jesus. I receive Gods overflowing grace and the gift of righteousness. And since I receive it by faith, I will reign in life through the one man Jesus Christ, the Messiah. My Savior already disarmed the powers and authorities. He made a public spectacle of them, triumphing over them by the cross. And since I am in Christ, I also triumph over all the enemy's works, not some, but all his works, schemes, wiles, tactics, and devices. In Jesus' Name. Amen!

SCRIPTURE REFERENCES

Revelation 5:10, Ecclesiastes 8:4, 2 Corinthians 2:14, Romans 8:37, 2 Corinthians 5:21, Romans 5:17, Colossians 2:15

Thought: Look how I deceived the whole world. What makes you so special? What makes you different from the rest? Answer: Shut Up Devil, it is written...

That these things were previously spoken unto me, therefore, I have peace in Christ. I understand that I will have tribulations in this world, but I'll be of good cheer as my savior, Jesus the Christ, The Messiah, has overcome the world. As it is written, the righteous person may have many troubles, but the Lord delivers him from them all. He doesn't deliver them from a few, but He delivers them from them all. Not to mention, He has sent forth heavenly resources and divine provision. As the angels of the Lord encamps around them, that fear him, and He delivers them. Yes!

True enough, the devil has deceived the whole world. As it is written, the great dragon- the ancient serpent called the devil, or Satan, the one deceiving the whole world, was thrown down to the earth with all his angels. But thanks be to God. Jesus disarmed all the powers and authorities and made a public spectacle of them, triumphing over them by the cross. And what makes me different from the rest is knowledge in the one in whom He sent. As it is written, my people are being destroyed for the lack of knowledge in me. But I know Him! And He is not ashamed to call me brother, as we are of the same family. Father God has made me a joint heir with Christ. And because I have been grafted in the family of God and a joint heir with Christ, I too am seated in heavenly places, far above principalities, powers, might, dominion, and every name that is named. This truth has been revealed to me by His Grace, and this revelation belongs to my children and me forever. As it is written, the secret things belong to the Lord our God, but what He reveals belongs to our children and us forever. In Jesus' Name. Amen!

SCRIPTURE REFERENCES

John 16:33, Psalms 34:19, Psalms 34:7, Revelations 12:9, Colossians 2:15, Hosea 4:6, Romans 8:17, Hebrews 2:11, Ephesians 1:21, Romans 11:19, Deuteronomy 29:29

Thought: You missed your opportunity. Answer: Shut Up Devil, it is written...

That God's Grace is more than sufficient for me. Has God run out of ways to bless me? Has He run out of mercies towards me? Has His grace peaked its limit? God forbids! He can make all grace, every favor and earthly blessing, come to me in abundance. I will always and under all circumstances and whatever the need, be self-sufficient. I didn't choose Him. He chose me before the foundations of the earth. As it is written, you didn't choose me. I chose you and ordained you to go and produce lasting fruit. Therefore, when I miss an opportunity. I rest in the truth that God still chose me before the foundations of the earth and didn't change his mind about me. I take hold of the abundant grace of God to provide another divine opportunity. I rest in the patience of my God. Not to lay a foundation of repentance but knowing that He is not slow to fulfill his promise as some count slowness but is patient toward me. He will never leave me nor forsake me. He will never give up on me or be angry with me. As it is written, there is, therefore, now no condemnation to them that are in Christ Jesus. In Jesus' Name. Amen!

SCRIPTURE REFERENCES

2 Corinthians 12:9, 2 Corinthians 9:8, John 15:16, 2 Peter 3:9, Hebrews 6:1, Deuteronomy 31:6, Isaiah 54:9, Romans 8:1

Thought: You can't manage all those ideas. All your ideas are scrambled in your head. You'll accomplish nothing! Answer: Shut Up Devil, it is written...

That I can do all things through Christ, which strengthens me; therefore, I'll be strong in the Lord and the power of His might, knowing that it is He who works through me and gives me my strength. As it is written, by strength shall no man prevail. But Christ in me is the Hope of Glory. I have understanding in the truth that it will not be me of myself to accomplish anything, lest any man should boast. But it will be God that keeps my feet and gives me strength. I will be accurate, thorough, and precise in writing my vision down. I will persevere in patience, knowing that after I've done the will of God, I will receive all that He has promised me. My vision and ideas are for an appointed time. As it is written, for the vision is yet for an appointed time, and it hastens to the end [fulfillment]; and it will not deceive or disappoint. And though it tarries, I will wait [earnestly] for it, because it will surely come; it will not be behindhand on its appointed day. Therefore, I will write my vision and ideas down plainly so that everyone who passes by will be able to carry the correct message to others. These ideas and visions come from the Lord. Since I know this truth, I also know that He always causes me to triumph in Christ. In Jesus' Name. Amen!

SCRIPTURE REFERENCES

Philippians 4:13, Ephesians 6:10, 1 Samuel 2:9,
Hebrews 10:36, Habakkuk 2:2-3, 2 Corinthians 2:14,
Colossians 1:27, Ephesians 2:9

Thought: You've done too much in your past to be forgiven.
Answer: Shut Up Devil, it is written...

That I have been crucified with Christ, and when a man dies, he is freed and delivered from the power of sin; therefore, if I have died with Christ, then I shall also live with him. No one can dare bring a charge against me. For it is God himself that justified me. We all have a past! As it is written, we all used to live in sin, just like the rest of the world, obeying the devil, who is the commander of the powers in the unseen world. He is the spirit at work in the hearts of those who refuse to obey God. All of us used to live that way, following the passionate desires and inclinations of our sinful nature. But God is so rich in mercy, and He loved me so much that even though I was dead because of my sins, He gave me life when He raised Christ from the dead. Therefore, it is only by God's grace that I have been saved. So, I don't boast in my good deeds nor become enslaved to my past. That old man has died. But now I'm a new creation altogether. As it is written, old things are passed away, and now all things have become new. I am a new creature in Christ! By the mercies of God, my past, present, and future sins have been taken out of the way and nailed to the cross. God remembers the sins no more because of that one man's sacrifice. So as far as the east is from the west, so far has He removed my transgressions from me. In Jesus' Name. Amen!

SCRIPTURE REFERENCES

Galatians 2:20, Romans 6:7-8, Romans 8:33,
Ephesians 2:2-5, 2 Corinthians 5:17, Hebrews 8:12,
Colossians 2:14, Psalms 103:12

Thought: You'll never get over what you've been through.
Answer: Shut Up Devil, it is written...

That my Heavenly Father blotted out my transgressions for His own sake and will remember my sins no more, my past has been blotted out by the Blood of Jesus and replaced with new memories of my righteousness in Christ. As it is written, the memory of the righteous is blessed. Everything I've been through is saturated by the Blood of my savior. Old things have passed away, and all things have become new. I now only use my past as a reference point, but never a place of residence. I learn from my past! As it is written, it was good for me to be afflicted so that I might learn your decrees. Therefore, I do not neglect or despise humble beginnings or what I've been through. But I embrace it as necessary towards my growth in Christ. Knowing the truth that all things work together for good to those who love God and are called according to his purpose. Nothing is too hard for God. He is more than able to make all grace come to me in abundance. I will forget those things which are behind me as I move forward to what's divinely positioned in front of me. As it is written, one thing I do is forget what is behind and press toward what is ahead. In Jesus' Name. Amen!

SCRIPTURE REFERENCES

Isaiah 43:25, proverbs 10:7, 2 Corinthians 5:17, Jeremiah 32:27, Philippians 3:13, Psalms 119:71, Zechariah 4:10, Romans 8:28

Thought: You'll never get out of prison. Answer: Shut Up Devil, it is written...

That this is the acceptable year of the Lord, this is the time of the Lord's favor. Prison is not my portion. He came for all who mourn, for the Lord came to set the captives free. As it is written, The Spirit of the Lord is upon me, for the Lord has anointed me to bring good news to the poor. He has sent me to comfort the brokenhearted and proclaim that captives will be released and prisoners will be freed. The Lord's arm is not waxed short, and you will see whether what I'm saying will come true for me because I believe! And as it is written, If you can believe, all things are possible to him who believes. And I believe! That is my portion! For I am the redeemed of the Lord. He has redeemed my life from destruction. I've been bought with a price. Yes, I have sinned! Yes, I have done evil deeds to land me in prison. But that man has died. Old things have passed away, and now all things have become new. As it is written, all have sinned and fallen short of the Glory of God. In Jesus' Name. Amen!

SCRIPTURE REFERENCES

Isaiah 61:1, Number 11:23, Romans 3:23, Mark 9:23, Psalms 103:4, 1 Corinthians 6:20, 2 Corinthians 5:17,

Thought: God can't use you, you are damaged goods.
Answer: Shut Up Devil, it is written...

That His grace is all I need, and his power works best in my weakness; therefore, I take pleasure in my weaknesses and in the insults, hardships, persecutions, and troubles that I suffer for Christ because when I am weak, I am strong. Therefore, I'll be strong in the Lord and the power of His might. Not my might, but His might! Get behind me, Satan! Damaged goods may be what the world says, but God calls me victorious and more than a conqueror. It comes to my remembrance that Jesus was also the stone that the builders rejected. Yet, He became the cornerstone. God chooses the damaged, discarded, rejected, and forgotten. As it is written, God chose things that the world considers foolish to shame those who think they are wise. And He chose things that are powerless to shame those who are powerful. God chose things despised by the world, things counted as nothing at all, and used them to bring to nothing that the world considers important. God wanted it this way so no one can ever boast in His presence. God specializes in damaged goods. In Jesus' Name. Amen!

SCRIPTURE REFERENCES

1 Corinthians 1:27-29, 2 Corinthians 12:9-10,
Ephesians 6:10, Psalms 118:21-22, Romans 8:37

Thought: If I tricked you before, I'll trick you again.
Answer: Shut Up Devil, it is written...

That the thief comes to steal, kill, and destroy, but my Savior has come that I might have the abundant life. This is the life full of joy and peace in Christ until it overflows; therefore, let the thief steal no longer! In times past, I was deceived the same way the whole world is deceived, lacking knowledge. But now I know the truth! I know that outside of Christ, I can do nothing in my strength. As it is written, by strength shall no man prevail, and apart from Christ, I can do nothing. But likewise, with Him, I can do all things through Christ who strengthens me. I now have the understanding about abiding in the true vine and remaining in Him. As it is written, anyone who does not remain in Him is thrown away like a useless branch and withers. These types of branches are picked up, thrown into the fire, and burned. But, by staying connected to Christ, I will not be deceived by the evil one because daily, my flesh will be bound as my slave from its passions and desires. And my spirit will be loosed with full reign. As it is written, if we live in the spirit, let us also walk in the spirit. Therefore, I'm fully prepared to put on the whole armor of God, that I may be able to stand against the wiles, tactics, schemes, and plots of deception that come from the devil in the evil day. In Jesus' Name. Amen!

SCRIPTURE REFERENCES

John 10:10, Ephesians 4:28, Hosea 4:6, 1 Samuel 2:9.
John 15:5-6, Philippians 4:13, Galatians 5:25, Ephesians 6,11;13

Thought: You don't really believe everything in that book, do you? It doesn't even make sense. Answer: Shut Up Devil, it is written...

That the just shall live by faith, the journey I take is by faith and not by sight (senses, or appearance); therefore, I regulate my life and conduct myself by my convictions and beliefs. To believe means to have unqualified committal, and I believe God! Just as Abraham believed God. As it is written, Abraham believed God, and it was counted unto him as righteous because of his faith. Get behind me, Satan! Because what if some did not believe and were without faith? Do their lack of faith and their faithlessness nullify and make ineffective and void the faithfulness of God and His fidelity to His Word? Of course not! By no means! Let God be found true and every human being a liar. I rest in the truth that God is Holy, and He cannot lie. For me to deny His word is me denying God Himself. He and His word are one. As it is written, in the beginning, was the word, and the word was with God, and the Word was God. Just as God is a faith and cannot be intellectualized, His word cannot be intellectualized but must be revealed.

As it is written, the secret things belong to the Lord our God, but those revealed belong to our children and us forever. Get behind me, Satan! You must be born again for the spirit of wisdom and understanding to flow with revelation knowledge. As it is written, when the disciples came to Jesus and asked, "Why do you speak to the people in parables?" He replied and said unto them: Because it has been given to you to know the mysteries of the kingdom of heaven, but to them, it has not been given. The word of God does not make sense; it makes faith! As God is a faith God, so is His word. In Jesus' Name. Amen!

SCRIPTURE REFERENCES

Romans 1:17, 2 Corinthians 5:7, Romans 3:3-4, Titus 1-2, John 1:1, Deuteronomy 29:29, Matthew 13:10-11, Romans 4:3, John 3:3

Thought: You see how many people are dying! COVID/CANCER/DISEASE is going around and YOU'RE GOING TO CATCH IT! Answer: Shut Up Devil, it is written...

That no weapon formed against me shall prosper, and every tongue that rises against me in judgment, I will condemn it; therefore, right now! In the name of Jesus, I come against the formed weapon of COVID, and I condemn its risen judgment against me. I've been purchased at a high price! I've been redeemed! And my redemption includes my body. My body has already been presented as a living sacrifice to God. I've been translated into the Kingdom of His dear son and now a moving organism within the body of Christ. And there is no sickness or infirmity of any kind in the body of Christ. This is my heritage as a son of the living God, who serves within the Kingdom of God. My righteousness is of God, whom I'm in everlasting covenant with. Therefore, a thousand shall fall at my side, and ten thousand at my right hand; but it shall not come near me.

I've been redeemed from destruction and crowned with His loving kindness and tender mercies. As it is written, surely, He will save me from the fowler's snare and the deadly pestilence because He is my refuge, my fortress, and my defense. Because He has given His angels charge over me to keep me in all my ways, I can rest with his truth as my shield and buckler that no evil shall befall me; neither shall any plague come near my house. Get behind me, Satan! Just as quick as the weapon is formed or the plague touches this body, it must die instantly because of the burden removing, yoke destroying the anointing power of God. As it is written, touch not my anointed, and do my prophets no harm. In Jesus' Name. Amen!

SCRIPTURE REFERENCES

Isaiah 54:17, Colossians 1:13-14, 1 Corinthians 6:20, Romans 12:1, Psalms 91:2;3;4;7;10, Jeremiah 32:40, Isaiah 10:27, Psalms 105:15 Psalms 103:4, Psalms 94:22

66 Books & 66 Thoughts!

"Contending in battle with the Word of God
is necessary for daily triumph."

~Karim Z. Henry

www.ingramcontent.com/pod-product-compliance
Lightning Source LLC
Chambersburg PA
CBHW021844130726
47989CB00009B/3084